The Great Pyramid

Gare Thompson

Contents

Ancient Egypt

Travel back to a time over 4,500 years ago. You are in a land called Egypt. It is in the northern part of Africa. Here it is very hot and dry.

Most people in **ancient** Egypt lived along the Nile River just as they do today.

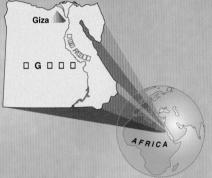

People have lived along the Nile River for thousands of years.

Ancient Egyptians created some amazing things. They made **mummies**. They invented a kind of writing called **hieroglyphics**. They made paper from a tall water plant called **papyrus**.

hieroglyphics

papyrus

One of the most amazing creations was the **pyramid**. It was a special kind of building. Each of the four sides of the pyramid was shaped like a triangle. The sloping sides came to a point at the top. This is the story of the greatest pyramid of them all.

The three largest pyramids in ancient Egypt were built at Giza.

The Great Pyramid at Giza
▲▲▲

▲ The largest pyramid ever built.

▲ Originally 481 feet (147 meters) high. This is as tall as a 33-story building.

▲ Covers an area of about 7 city blocks.

▲ Built with over 2,300,000 blocks of stone.

▲ Each stone weighed over 2 tons.

Why Did the Egyptians Build Pyramids?

The pyramids were **tombs**. Each was built to protect the body of a ruler of ancient Egypt. Ancient Egyptians believed that their spirit went on living in the land of the dead after they died. But to live forever, the spirit needed a body to rest in.

So, ancient Egyptians invented a way to **preserve** a dead body by making it into a mummy. The mummy of the dead ruler was placed in the pyramid.

The mummy was kept in a secret room within the pyramid.

To make a mummy, ancient Egyptians followed a number of steps. First, they took out all body parts except the heart. Next, they dried the body out with a special kind of salt. Then, they wrapped the body with many layers of cloth and covered the face with a mask. Finally, they placed the mummy in a wooden coffin, or box, shaped like a human body.

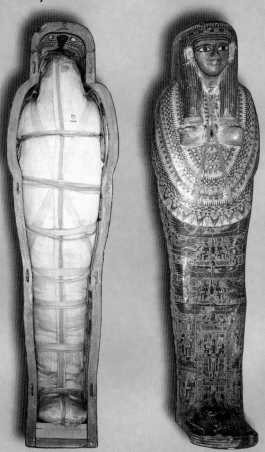

Ancient Egyptians tried to make the wooden coffin look like the living person.

Khufu

In ancient Egypt, the ruler was called **pharaoh**. The ancient Egyptians worshiped the pharaoh as a god on Earth. They built pyramids for many pharaohs. The largest pyramid was built for the pharaoh Khufu, who ruled ancient Egypt over 4,500 years ago.

Statue of Khufu

Khufu built his pyramid on the west side of the Nile River. Khufu began building his pyramid when he became pharaoh. He wanted to build the largest pyramid of all. He thought this would show he was the strongest ruler. Khufu's pyramid became known as the Great Pyramid at Giza.

Khufu's pyramid was the largest of the three pyramids at Giza.

Who Built the Great Pyramid?

Building a pyramid took a long, long time. It took 20 years or more to build the Great Pyramid. Many experts think that as many as 20,000 men helped to build it. Most of the workers were farmers when they were not working on the pyramid.

The Farmers

In ancient Egypt, most men were farmers. They lived and farmed along the Nile River. The Nile River flooded every year from June to September. The flooding helped make the soil along the Nile good for planting crops.

During the four months of flooding, farmers could not work in their fields. It was during these months that the farmers worked on the pyramid. Then, in October, when it was time to plant their crops, the farmers returned home. In June, when the floods came, they returned to work on the pyramids.

Egyptian farmers planted wheat and barley in the rich soil along the banks of the Nile River.

Skilled Workers

Some workers who built the pyramids were not farmers. These workers had special skills. The skilled workers stayed and worked on the pyramid all year.

Architects designed the pyramid. They drew the plans to show how the pyramid would look. They worked with **surveyors**. Surveyors made very careful measurements. They measured the sides of the pyramid with a plumb line. Each side of the pyramid had to be 756 feet (231 meters) long. The sides had to meet at the top.

An Egyptian worker used a plumb line to make sure each block of stone was straight.

The pyramids were built of white limestone. Stone **masons** cut the stones into building blocks. Each block of stone weighed over two tons. They measured each stone carefully. Measuring was very important. The sides had to be straight. Each stone had to fit into its place on the pyramid. If one stone were off by only a tiny amount, the other stones would not fit. Another group of skilled workers was the metal workers. Metal workers made and sharpened the tools that were used to build the pyramids.

Workers used chisels and mallets to cut limestone blocks. Polishing stones were used to give the stones a smooth finish.

polishing stone

copper chisel

wood mallet

How Was the Great Pyramid Built?

Moving the Stones

Workers did not have the wheel or the pulley to move the heavy stones. They did not have iron tools or machines. These things had not been invented yet. They used only simple machines and hard work to build the huge pyramid.

Workers were divided into groups. After the masons cut the stones, groups of workers dragged the stones from the **quarries** to ships. First, they made a path of logs leading to the ships. Then, they watered the paths to make them slippery. Finally, they tied ropes around the heavy stones and dragged them to ships that would carry them to the pyramid **site**.

Ships crossed the Nile and docked near the site. Work began again. Groups of workers made paths from the ship to the site. They watered the paths. They tied ropes around the stones and hauled the stones to the site.

Workers moved the heavy stones on paths paved with logs.

Building the Base

Before workers could build the pyramid they had to prepare the site. The site had to be as flat as a pancake. The workers smoothed the desert sand and removed any big stones.

Then, the workers built the base, or bottom, of the pyramid. They needed a long time to finish it. The base of the pyramid was about seven city blocks. The workers saw the pyramid slowly begin to take shape.

Building the Sides

Once the base was done, the workers began to work on the sides. To work on the sides, the workers built long ramps of mud and brick. They used ropes to haul the stones up the ramps.

Slowly, the workers dragged each stone up the ramp. They lowered each stone into its spot and slid it into place. Masons checked each stone to make sure it fit. All of the stones had to fit like pieces in a puzzle. If one stone didn't fit, it would throw off the whole pyramid.

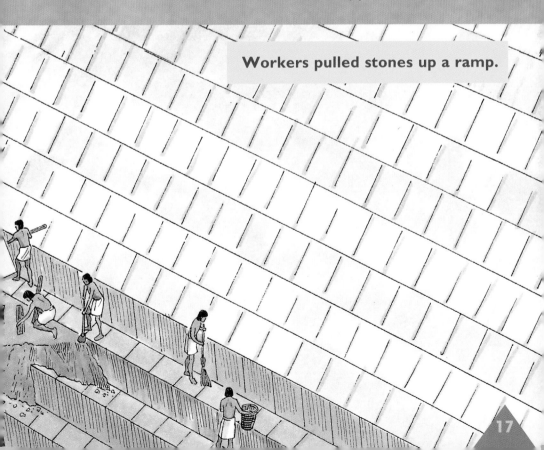

Workers pulled stones up a ramp.

The Finishing Touches

After many years, workers finally reached the top of the fourth side. At the very top of the pyramid, they placed the **capstone**. The capstone was shaped like a small pyramid. The capstone of the Great Pyramid shone in the sun like gold.

Workers placed a pyramid-shaped capstone on top of the pyramid.

Pyramid Facts

Some people believe that the original capstone may have been made of gold. No one knows for sure. Today, there is no gold top. If there was one once, then it is likely that robbers took it long ago.

Once the top was in place, workers added casing stones to the outside of the pyramid. The casing stones made the surface of the pyramid flat and smooth. Then workers polished the stones until they shone. When the last stone was polished, the pyramid sparkled in the sun. The outside was done. Now it was time to work on the inside.

From far away, the pyramid looked like it had been made out of one big white stone.

Inside the Pyramid

Several rooms and hallways were built inside the pyramid. The rooms were burial places for the ruler and his family. Artists painted and carved the inside of the pyramid. Some artists painted the columns. Others carved flowers or palm trees on the columns. Artists made statues of the pharaoh. The statues were placed inside the pyramid.

Workers filled the tomb with the things the pharaoh needed for his next life. They placed dishes, clothes, jewelry, furniture, and food in the tomb. Many of the items were made of gold, including the pharaoh's coffin.

The Great Pyramid was finished at last. Khufu now had the largest tomb ever built.

Workers decorated the inside of the pyramid and filled it with many treasures.

The Great Pyramid Today

The Great Pyramid has changed over time. Today, it is shorter than when it was first built. Sand and wind have worn down the top. The casing stones are gone. Robbers stole some of them. People used others in new buildings. Robbers also took many of the pharaoh's things. All that they left in the pharaoh's tomb was an empty coffin.

Many people visit the Great Pyramid today. Even empty, it is still a fascinating place. Visiting the Great Pyramid is like stepping back in time. We are just as amazed by it today as the first visitors were 4,500 years ago.

Glossary

ancient   very old; having existed long ago

architect   a person who designs buildings

capstone   the pyramid-shaped stone placed on the
                 very top of a pyramid

hieroglyphics   symbols and pictures that represent sounds,
                 words, and ideas

mason   a worker who builds with stones

mummy   a dead body preserved with special salts
                 and wrapped in cloth

papyrus   paper made from the stems of a tall water
plant that grows in northern Africa

pharaoh   ruler of ancient Egypt

preserve   to keep from decaying

pyramid   an ancient Egyptian stone monument where
                 pharaohs and their treasures were buried

quarry   a place where stones are dug from
                 the ground

site   the location where something is built

surveyor   a person who measures building sites

tomb   a grave, room, or building for holding
                 a dead body

Index